Dear Educators and Guardians,

Today's school music standards dictate that children should generate their own musical ideas. By joining Sir Dorian in the first of <u>The Valiant Quests of the Knights of Musical Acres</u>, readers have a great opportunity to stimulate musical thinking. When asked what kind of music should be made, consider all your choices. To which instruments do you have access? Are you inspired by classical, rap, jazz or rock-and-roll?

If it's rap, you could pull out drums or digital music apps and think about a favorite song to come up with ideas. For country music, perhaps you need a banjo or guitar, tambourine or a popsicle stick harmonica. Is it classical? Sit down at a piano or with a wind instrument – recorders can be fun for this!

Should learning a new instrument be prohibitive, try using digital music apps to simulate and record musical ideas. This Quest with Sir Dorian asks you to consider what steps need to be taken to make your music be heard. Do you need to come up with lyrics? Do you need to learn a new style of music? Today, it is possible – more than ever before – to discover music in so many forms, and create your own songs! And the best part: the next time you read the book you can make a different kind of music. You might also find the cards included helpful for getting started.

Kids are amazingly open to what they can accomplish. Read them this book. Open the door to making new music! It's possible that you, along with them, end up down a musical road you never expected to take, discovering a love for creating music in your noble quest to help Sir Dorian. And, fear not! There are more knights, coming soon!

Dawn-Marie Schafer

Music Educator
Austin, TX

*Having an idea and turning it into a book IS as hard as it sounds.
The experience is both challenging and rewarding. But, the world is a better place
thanks to people who want to come alongside others for the benefit of children.
I especially want to thank the individuals that helped make this book happen:
Dr. Mickey Kolis, former Education Professor at the University of Wisconsin-Eau Claire for
inspiring this book through his own vision for rethinking teaching; Jonathan Aseron, working
with you has been pure excitement - your work gave this book life and made my year;
Dr. Tom Leonard, Superintendent of Eanes ISD in Austin, TX for believing in and sharing our
project; Kelly Dunning, EISD Art teacher for her expertise with layout, formatting, editing, and
friendship; Dale Baker, EISD Digital Art teacher for help with scanning the illustrations.*

*I'd like to thank my husband John for not only his support and feedback, but for being
as excited about it as I am and our children Hannah, Jonah & Selah for their
enthusiasm and support!*

~ Dawn-Marie

*I'd like to thank my family for always being supportive of my artistic endeavors,
and my boys for drawing alongside me during the making of this book!*

~ Jonathan

The Valiant Quests of the Knights of
MUSICAL ACRES
Quest 1: Sir Dorian's Dilemma

... because no one should grow up without having played their own songs.

Written by
Dawn-Marie Schafer

Illustrated by
Jonathan Aseron

Meet Sir Dorian,

Grand Knight of Musical Acres!

The majestic Kingdom of
Musical Acres was filled with a
symphony of sound;
birds singing, crickets chirping,
and trees clapping, as clouds
floated by on the
whistling breeze.

And Sir Dorian?

He loved all the beautiful sounds
of Musical Acres.

He sang along with Bluebird,
and hummed with Cricket.

He added his drumming to the
rhythms of the woods.

He strummed his guitar,
and joined his
friends in serenading the
open skies each day!

At night he played his trumpet for the moon, while his friend Frog croaked along.

Accompanied by his friends of the forest, the young knight created his very own songs each and every day!

Like every other peaceful, beautiful morning, this one began when Sir Dorian woke, donned his armor, and set out for a fun day of Knighting and musicking in Musical Acres.

But then he heard it.
He stopped in his tracks!
It was the sound of...

SILENCE.

He could not believe his ears!
Musical Acres had never been
silent before!
Where were his friends?
Bluebird? Cricket? Frog?

The river was dry!

Now Sir Dorian needs
our help filling Musical Acres
with music once again!

It's time for a

What kind of music
should we make in our quest
to help Sir Dorian find his friends
and fill the air with sound?

What do we
need to gather
to make our
musical ensemble?

Think about all the
steps you will need to take
to create your music.

Now get started!

YOU get to fill the land with
music of your own making,
and soon...

Musical Acres

will be musical again

thanks to you!

These friends made our book possible,

Thank you!

Doc, Stella & Jun Aseron & Family

Hudson Barras & Family

Bossie Family

Rick & Pam Bronson

Brooklyn Byrd & Family

Jennifer Champagne

Elizabeth Compton

Kristen Donaldson

Connie Graham & Chuck Chatraw

Colton Harbert

Jennifer Ice

Nicole Livet

Jeffrey & Breeze Marsh

Benjamin & Katherine McDonnell & Family

Lisa Miller

Sharon O'Donnell

Valor, Merit & Atlas O'Mahoney and
Hardy & Fenix Willett & Family

Ron & Cynthia Pettigano

Jackie & Maria Ramos & Family

Bennett & Campbell Ruback & Family

Elizabeth Sands

Heather Sheffield

Julia Webber

Dawn-Marie Schafer
Author

Off of my Grandfather's piano bench, through the music classrooms and research libraries at the Hartt School of Music and Boston University College of Fine Arts into your corner of the world, I bring a life-long passion for music, people, and writing to spark your favorite kid's creativity for music composition. Originally a New Jersey girl, Austin, Texas is now home to my family of five. My newest classrooms full of kids are reading this book and learning that making their own music is fresh and exciting! I love your kids as much as I love my own and this book – well, it's for all of them.

Jonathan Aseron
Illustrator

I was born and raised in Statesboro, Georgia. After receiving a BFA degree in painting and drawing from the University of Georgia, I attended the University of Texas for graduate school. I earned a MFA degree in 2009 in studio art. I am currently an art teacher at Eanes Elementary School in Austin, Texas. I live with my wife, Tara, and my twin sons, Theo and Louie. Other than hanging out with my family, I love to make art, write music, and be outside in my spare time.